The Sell-Off on Wall Street

B T

Copyright © 2020 by B T

First published as, Six Days of Selling, 15th May 2020.

All rights reserved. Not to be copied or distributed in any way without the publisher's permission. No part of this book may be reproduced in any form without permission in writing from the publisher. For information visit the publisher's website. This book is written as a source of information only, and it should not be considered a substitute for the advice, decisions, or judgment of the reader's professional advisors. Every reader's situation is different, and readers should seek professional advice before making any investment decisions. The reader is responsible for his or her own actions. Neither the author nor the publisher assumes any responsibility or liability whatsoever on behalf of the purchaser or reader of these materials. Any perceived slight of any individual or organization is purely unintentional.

Printed in the United States of America.

Paperback ISBN: 979-8-3378-1289-2

Table of Contents

1: FASTEST WALL STREET CRASH 7

2. STIMULUS FOR THE ECONOMY 12

3. MONEY, INFLATION, & GROWTH IMPACTS 17

4. 2020: INDUSTRY ANALYSIS 22

5. A GLOBAL SELL-OFF 28

6. FINANCIAL MARKETS REBOUND 31

7: HISTORICAL FINANCIAL CRISES 34

8: 2022: A NASDAQ CORRECTION 39

APPENDIX 41

ABOUT THE AUTHOR 63

BIBLIOGRAPHY 64

INTRODUCTION

In early 2020, between February and March the stock market entered a historic crash. Soon the fear had spread across the global financial markets, and the resulting sell-off was the fastest ever recorded on Wall Street, and six trillion dollars wiped from global indices over a period of six days.

Find the answers to important questions including, why did the stock market crash? What happened to investments? What does it mean for the economy? Is investors' money safe in the stock market?

An easy-to-follow guide on the 2020 financial markets crash. Included inside, financial charts, the latest economic data, historical comparisons (2008), and market commentary. Suggested for readers interested in topics including economics, finance, financial crises, money, investing, & Wall Street. Plus, includes the cryptocurrency crash 2022, 2023 U.S. banking crisis, and the collapse of Credit Suisse.

Updated and revised edition.
Enjoy reading, The Sell-Off on Wall Street by B T

1: FASTEST WALL STREET CRASH

In late February 2020, $6 trillion dollars was wiped from global markets in just six trading days, according to market data by S&P Dow Jones Indices. Never had such large sums of money been lost in such a short period.

During February 2020 the financial markets started to drop on news reports of the Coronavirus (later called, Covid-19) spreading. Market participants continued to sell stocks and other investments all at once on Wall Street, the trading screens used by investors around the world flashed red for days, as the stock prices plunged lower. The computer trading systems and stop-loses trading strategies likely triggered more selling. Such a broad-based sell-off shocked investors around the world. At this point, it seemed nothing could stop the crash.

During the Bull* market since March 9, 2009, to February 19, 2020, the S&P 500 had soared 400.5%. The longest Bull market in history which had followed the 2008 financial crisis, had ended with a crash in early 2020. It changed from Bull to a Bear Market

The decline on the major Wall Street indexes were immediate: The S&P 500 composite (an index of 500 US stocks) recorded the fastest correction -10% in Wall Street history, from a market high on the 19th of February to the 27th of February, declined (-12%), (see, Exhibits 1-5). Circuit breakers were used to pause the stock market during the sell-off (see Appendix, i). Many investors likely began to question if their money was safe in the stock market?

Global markets also declined in the sell-off. All major international indexes recorded large percentage drops during this period, for more (see, Chapter 5). Especially after seeing large losses in their portfolios, and investment accounts, similarly this had happened in 2008. There were also published reports of traders who had successfully shorted the market and made large gains from the trade.

Volatility during trading was very high in February and March 2020, and this is shown by the VIX chart (see, Appendix #2) and the volatility in trading during Feb-March 2020 is highlighted below showing some of the most volatile trading days, with wild moves both up and down by 9% or more on the Dow Jones Industrial Average (DJIA), (see Appendix, ii) DJIA). The Russell 2000 index also fell sharply with the smaller listed companies being less safe during the crash, and more exposed to an economic downturn. Bets on volatility

(VIX Index) linked products also delivered spectacular returns like *TVIX, see* (Author's note).

How did the safe-haven investments perform in early 2020? The stock market crash in 2020 increased the demand for safe-haven investments. They include asset classes like gold, bonds, Treasuries, currencies, & cash, were all active during the stock market crash, with mixed performances based on historical comparisons. It was a challenging period for safe-haven investments because they didn't perform as expected initially, and were not as stable due to the volatility. These investments mostly bounced back from losses after dropping (except bonds), also (see, Appendix, iv).

Different industry sectors were perceived by investors to be too risky in the crash, new travel restrictions impacted on travel related stocks like airlines, and cruise ships. Restrictions on movement (lockdowns) were a challenge particularly for retail and travel related stocks. Banks like J.P. Morgan which is considered a bellwether* for the American economy declined, alongside other financial firms during the crash. Many firms subsequently stopped providing forwards earnings estimates, and stopped dividend payments to investors, due to the uncertainty caused by the economic downturn.

The stock market crash that started in early 2020, saw new stimulus support and actions by the Federal Reserve to provide liquidity (new money), and to provide confidence to financial markets, for more (see Chapter 2). On 23 March 2020, the S&P 500 reached a low point in its sell-off and was down 34% from the peak.

Investors' confidence in the financial markets had been tested between February and March 2020. The decline in equities in early 2020 broke records for the speed and size of the crash. It raised many questions for market participants. How much longer would the markets continue to fall?

This chapter reviews the 2020 financial crash. In late February 2020, $6 trillion dollars was lost from global markets in just six days, and it was the fastest correction -10% drop ever recorded on Wall Street in history.

Footnote:
*A bull market is when the stock market rises for an extended period, a bear market is the opposite, when it falls. Market sentiment is said to be either bullish or bearish.

*Wall Street is used as a common term to describe the U.S. financial markets, many firms are located on Wall Street including the New York Stock Exchange, where stocks are traded.

*The VelocityShares Daily 2X VIX Short-Term ETN (TVIX), this was an exchange-traded note (ETN) that followed the CBOE Volatility Index (VIX), 200% leverage on daily volatility changes, issued by Credit Suisse Securities (CS). (TVIX) soared during February 2020 as volatility went up suddenly. According to media reports the product was de-listed in June 2020.

2. STIMULUS FOR THE ECONOMY

During March 2020, the Federal Reserve acted quickly, it started easing and launched initiatives to support the markets. On 12 March the Federal Reserve made $500 billion available for overnight funding operations, and repo operations totaling $1 trillion on 13 Friday, 2020[i]. This was evidence that liquidity was becoming scarce in some markets. Quantitative easing (is the purchase of US Treasuries) and "unlimited" asset purchases (having already exceeded a $700billion cap) by the US Federal Reserve was rolled out, and the real economy started to show worrying signs of a recession. The total money committed by the Federal Reserve for support, was estimated to be $6 trillion dollars, for credit and lending programs[ii]. Wall Street had been bailed out again in 2020.

Support via stimulus and guarantees of stability, are expected to provide stability, especially during a period of a financial market crash like during the 2020 crash, and/or a recession. If capital becomes scarcer then liquidity problems can lead to companies' bankruptcy, defaulted loans, a credit contraction, and a banking crisis. In the worst-case scenario, this is what central banks try to prevent from happening. Trust in the financial system should not fail. But history tells us it can and past financial crises are a warning for what can happen during a sell-off.

During the 2008 financial crisis there was a massive stimulus programme in the United States, and money way injected into the financial system, via a term called 'quantitative easing', and toxic debt was brought by the Federal Reserve, to support the banks and restore confidence. This was essentially a bailout of Wall Street, and many Main Street businesses failed, also see TARP (Chapter 7).

Further, the House passed a number of stimulus measures to support the economy, including:

- The CARES Act passed at the end of March provided $2.2 trillion dollars, it provided paycheck protection for small businesses, stimulus cheques for Americans ($1,200 per individual), unemployment benefis, a corporate bailout fund, aid for hospitals and money for state and local governments.

- The Heroes Act a $3 Trillion tax cut and the spending bill passed on 15 March, 2020. It continued the support for business, individuals, and the states.[iii]

Stimulus was used to restore confidence to the financial markets during this period. The effect of widespread stimulus distorts the prices in the financial markets, and this could lead to a new crash when the support is withdrawn. Continued use of stimulus can be expected to support financial markets.

<u>Zero interest rate:</u>

The federal funds rate the short-term interest rate the central bank charges bank for lending was reduced to support lending (see below). Two swift cuts were made to cut the interest rate to zero, in an unprecedented move to support the financial system, and stop a credit contraction from damaging the economy. Zero interest rates make the dollar less attractive relative to other currencies with a higher yield, and this could lead to a dollar crash!

Federal Funds Rate Actions:

- March 03, 2020. Reduces the federal funds rate by 1/2 percentage point, to 1 to 1 1/4 percent

- March 15, 2020. Drops the federal funds rate to 0 to 1/4 percent.

On 15 May, in response to a question about negative interest rates, the central bank chief, Jerome Powel said, "I know there are fans of the policy, but for now it's not something that we're considering."[iv] Negative interest rates have been used before for example in Japan, which started using negative interest rates in 2016 to encourage growth, and because of high debt levels. The carry trade* is a popular strategy for Wall Street funds, and institutions to profit from the low interest rates available by borrowing in the Japanese Yen.

Footnote:

*A carry trade is when borrowing occurs at a low-interest rate to invest in a currency, or product with a higher interest rate.

Negative interest rates would an unusual move should they be used by the Federal Reserve[v], and they may well use them in the future. The consequences of negative interest rates could be hard to anticipate, and it would mean savers would receive a negative return on their bank deposits. Cash deposits are insured up to a limited amount in the U.S.

This chapter outlines some of the early actions taken by the U.S. government and the Federal Reserve in 2020. Stimulus was used to provide support to the markets and the amount used was at historic levels.

3. MONEY, INFLATION, & GROWTH IMPACTS

There were signs of trouble in the US economy before the stock market crash occurred. For example, there was deficits and an increasing debt load being added to the U.S. governments books, Debt-to-GDP was at close to 80% before the stock market crash, and that was double the level before the financial crisis of 2008.[vi]

The developments of purchasing more Treasuries in 2020 would further increase the money supply, and the introduction of zero interest rates, had likely increased the expectation of higher inflation in 2020, the dollar risked being devalued by these decisions. The gold backing of the dollar was stopped in 1968, which increased the amount of credit in the financial system to an almost unlimited degree.

Money Supply

The money supply has been expanded rapidly since 2008, as the Federal Reserve continued to monetize government borrowing by buying the debt issued to finance spending, the money in circulation doubled since 2008.[vii] The M2 Money Supply in 2020 rose since the start of 2020 to 17.57 trillion during May, from 14.57 trillion from one year ago.[viii]

Inflation Risk

Inflation occurs when consumer prices increase, and the purchasing power of the dollar declines. By increasing the money supply the Federal Reserve risked high inflation and devaluing the dollar. The United States has seen periods of high inflation in the past, for example the 1970s was a period of high inflation. Consumer demand for goods and services can also impact on the inflation rate. If consumers do not spend as much during the recession, then consumer prices may fall to compensate for the reduced demand.

Deflation is the opposite of inflation. The consumer prices decline, and the purchasing power of the dollar increases, if consumer demand falls then consumer prices can collapse. For example, the oil price collapsed following lower demand in 2020.

Inflation/Hyperinflation Risk

A lesson on the dangers from printing money can be found in what happened in Germany in the 1920s, when there was hyperinflation. To make war reparations payments, the German mark was devalued by printing marks, and the resulting hyperinflation resulted in citizens life savings becoming worthless marks.[ix] A recent example of hyperinflation was seen in Zimbabwe, were printed bills were worth billions, but worth very little in real terms. The risk of hyperinflation or just inflation is a real risk to the financial system.

Growth Forecast

Economic growth was likely reduced following the stock market crash in 2020. The bank Goldman Sachs, issued an early growth forecast for GDP (Gross Domestic Product) with the following projections: for the first 3 months of 2020 was 0%, for the second quarter -0.5% contraction, and for the third quarter 3%.[x] How badly the economy will be impacted by the lockdown, and Covid-19 pandemic? At the time of writing, it is not clear, economic growth in the United States in 2020 could decline much more than forecast, and could decline anywhere from 5%-20%, or more.

Recession Risks

A recession is a period when economic activity declines and unemployment rises. The Federal Reserve quickly lowered the short-term interest rate, and pumped liquidity into the markets with stimulus programs in an effort to stop the stock market crash from damaging the financial system. From mid-March, the unemployment rate had surged to 14.7%, and one in five Americans or 36.5 million people had filed for unemployment. The U.S. economy had lost 20.5 million jobs.[xi]

Many companies filed for bankruptcy following the sell-off, including the discount retailer, J.C. Penny. Many companies declined to provide forwards earning guidance, and this showed how uncertain the market was. A recession would have a long-lasting impact on the economy and have a significant impact on financial markets.

Also, the policy action by the Federal Reserve and government to support economic activity may shorten the impact of the recession in the United States.

This chapter discusses the dollar value, money supply, inflation, and growth expectations in 2020. Significant pressures on inflation and growth following the stimulus, and changes in demand in the economy have been forecasted. Money supply had been increasingly for a long period before the crash.

4. 2020: INDUSTRY ANALYSIS

Industry sectors had to adjust to the challenges of Covid-19, and new restrictions. The change in economic activity and travel restrictions presented a challenge for many industries. Supply chains were disrupted globally as countries went into lockdown. Consumers were required to stay-at-home, and international travel stopped due to the spread of the Coronavirus. Hard hit sectors included: travel, retail, healthcare & financials. Biotechnology and information technology companies bounced back strongly on Wall Street.

Retail Industry

The retail sector is made up of retail stores. Panic buying during February and March saw many grocery retailers left with empty shelves as customers purchased sanitiser, toilet paper, and other household supplies in preparation. Retail stores have been impacted by the pandemic, and the sector saw some companies enter bankruptcy. On 13 March 2020, Apple closed its retail stores.[xii] On 15 May 2020, J.C. Penney Co Inc filed for bankruptcy protection.[xiii]

Travel Industry

The travel sector is made up of companies including airlines, hotels and cruise line companies. Companies in the travel sector encountered serious issues, and customers stopped traveling. The decline in earnings for these companies challenged the viability of many companies. Airlines in the United States received support from the government.

On 2nd May 2020, Berkshire Hathaway an investment company held it's shareholder meeting virtually for the first time, the world's best investor Warren Buffet the chairman announced he had sold a position worth billions, in four major airlines, "The world has changed for the airlines. And I don't know how it's changed, and I hope it corrects itself in a reasonably prompt way," Buffett said.[xiv]

Hertz* the rental car company was close to filing for bankruptcy (*at the time of writing*).

Footnote:

*Hertz became a Meme stock (a stock with a large following on social media) and was able to exit bankruptcy proceedings, GameStop another Meme stock went up 2,700% in January 2021.

The Cruise ship industry had several significant incidents early in 2020, and faced restrictions. The Diamond Princess had an outbreak of Covid-19 onboard and was quarantined off Japan for two weeks [xv], and the Ruby Princess had a similar outbreak onboard in Australia, both owned by Carnival Corporation. Also, other cruise operators had outbreaks during this period, and presented a major challenge. The cruise ship industry outlook is highly uncertain.

Financial Industry

The financial sector is made up of companies including banks, financial services, and insurance companies. Banking stocks were sold heavily during the stock market crash, as expectations of defaults increased. J. P. Morgan a large U.S. bank, which is a bellwether for the economy declined in price during the crash, also other large financial institutions.

Energy Industry

The energy sector saw a step decline in prices. The crash in the price of oil (the USO fund went into negative oil prices) caused losses for oil companies. The reason for the decline in prices can be attributed to expected lower demand for oil, as economic activity was likely to reduce the demand for oil. Other supply or market moves could also explain the decline.

Consumer Staples Industry

The consumer stables sector is made up of companies that produce food, and other household essentials. Manufacturing capabilities were impacted by supply chain disruptions, and lockdowns, which caused shortages in retailers. While companies in this sector are considered defensive because these items have stable demand, even during a recession, and stocks were stable.

Healthcare Industry

The sector is made up of hospitals and medical supply companies. The healthcare sector came under a huge amount of pressure in early 2020. Medical suppliers ran out of protective equipment, and hospitals face shortages of essentials. The sector benefited from funding from the government, and increased capital expenditure on medical supplies.

Demand for diagnostic products and services in the response to Covid-19. The immediate demand for PCR tests, and other rapid tests and services outpaced supply, and stocks in the industry soared. Some diagnostic companies offering tests on the stock market included, Labcorp, Quest Diagnostics, Co-Diagnostics, and Opko Health .

Information Technology Industry

The sector is made up of software, Internet services, and computing companies. Information technology was the top-performing sector on the stock market in early 2020. Companies in this sector are resilient due to their global customer base, online solutions, and new trends in business. More companies are moving their operations towards using information technology services like cloud computing, remote working, and video communication services, in response to the outbreak. A greater shift towards E-commerce was also beneficial.

Biotechnology Industry

The sector is made up of companies that make pharmaceuticals, vaccines, and other medicine. The search for a cure for the Coronavirus saw investment interest in the sector increase. Companies with promising vaccines rose in value during the pandemic.

A challenge for companies in this sector is the extended time it takes to find and develop a vaccine. During May 2020, the president started 'Operation Warp Speed', an initiative to speed up the development of a vaccine.

Public companies developing a vaccine or medicine for Covid-19 include Gilead, Moderna, Merck, University of Oxford, and Johnson & Johnson, Biontech, Arbutus Biopharma, Novavax.

This chapter reviews how industry sectors were impacted and responded to events in early 2020, some industries are more susceptible to the challenges while others benefited from changes in business operations and demand.

5. A GLOBAL SELL-OFF

The drop in equities was not confined to Wall Street in February and March 2020. The sell-off went global, with international markets recording massive declines, from Europe to Asia, the selling was broad and the losses reached trillions of dollars.

International Markets

Another financial crisis in the Eurozone! Following on from the 2008 financial crisis when in subsequent years the European Central Bank pumped billions into banks in the region to avert disaster, the ECB created a new round of stimulus to respond to the Coronavirus pandemic. Several countries including Italy, and Britain had recorded high number of fatalities from the health crisis.

On the 18th March 2020, the ECB announced stimulus of €750bn (£653bn) via bond purchases, it was authorized under the banner of the public sector purchase programme (PSPP), which caused some opposition from Germany over the legality of it.[xvi] The ECB said when announcing the stimulus, "To that end, the ECB will ensure that all sectors of the economy can benefit from supportive financing conditions that enable them to absorb this shock." The stimulus provided liquidity to banks and was another round of quantitative easing, this was effectively another bailout. Stimulus was also used as a response in Europe, and further abroad to support financial markets from declining further and support the economy.

Britain is planning to leave the Eurozone in 2020, and this development is known widely as Brexit, and it could lead to more uncertainty and instability, for financial stability in U.K, and Europe.

Australia was also caught in the global sell-off, on Monday March 9th, 2020 the ASX 200 dropped by 7.3 per cent, $137 billion, or 46 points, and ended the day at 5,822. The ASX 200 was down from the high it reached in February of 5,761, a $413 billion loss (*ABC NEWS*).

Footnote:

Lannin, S. 2020, "ASX crashes below 6,000 with almost $140b wiped off in worst day since global financial crisis", *ABC NEWS*, https://www.abc.net.au

Emerging markets were also sold during February and March 2020, as widely reported. Emerging markets have been more susceptible to economic downturns and capital flight in the past (see Asia Crisis 1997-1998), and this was the case again in 2020.

This chapter explains how the financial market crash was not confined to the United States but was a global financial crash in early 2020. Europe enacted large stimulus measures like the United States during this period. To avert a financial crisis.

6. FINANCIAL MARKETS REBOUND

Wall Street rebounded quickly after the low on 23 March 2020. From this point the stock market moved higher, with less volatility in trading, the daily -+9% moves that occurred in March 2020 had ended (see Exhibits, 6-8 in Appendix). The financial market crash had been stopped, and it seemed that an ongoing financial melt-down had been averted in early 2020.

Companies started to report decent earnings, and actions from the Federal Reserve and stimulus programs provided a floor to the markets. The panic and non-stop selling by traders was over and stability returned to Wall Street, and beyond. On 7 May 2020, the Nasdaq Composite Index turned positive for the year, it was a surprising rebound. Many market commentators began to ask why the markets were suddenly bullish again? Was there a divergence between Wall Street and Main Street? Only time will tell if the recovery in the stock market will last.

But by May (time of writing), the rebound was not complete for all indexes. Could the markets see another correction in the near future? Has the market really recovered, or is it only a temporary rebound?

If investors did not sell during the crash in late February, early March 2020 then losses could have been avoided as the Nasdaq Index rebounded, but many investors, funds, and institutions did sell during the crash and recorded significant losses. Also for those investors who brought during the low in March it presented a unique opportunity to profit from cheap stocks.

The cause of the market panic can be attributed to the emergence of a global pandemic in early 2020, and the financial markets and economy (at the time of writing) remain tied to the development of vaccines. Important questions have been answered in this guide including, why did the market crash? What happened to investments? What does it mean for the economy? Is investors' money safe in the stock market?

The 2020 financial crash/sell-off will continue to have longterm impacts on the financial markets on Wall Street and international markets, and the economy for a long period.

This chapter describes how financial markets in the United States and abroad staged a recovery following the Feb-March sell-off.

Completed writing, May 2020.

Author's note:

Updated, in 2021, the S&P 500 went up 26.9%, Dow Jones Industrial Average (DJIA) increased 18.7%, and the Nasdaq Composite gained 21.4% for the year. (Forbes)

7: HISTORICAL FINANCIAL CRISES

Throughout history there have been many financial crises/sell-offs/financial crashes. The boom and bust of the stock markets are nothing new, and early financial crises were often due to lack of regulation or other market failures. The earliest stock market crash was the Dutch Tulip Crash of 1600, in Holland, when the price of a single tulip rose to astronomical levels, before the tulip bubble burst, and many speculators lost their money.

While much can be learned from studying past financial crises, and stock market panics, every new stock market crash is different from those before it. The perils of the financial markets should be a reminder to investors of what can go wrong, when things start to fall apart. Today many protections are in-place to protect investors money, and in the early panics no such protections existed, while complex financial products caused the 2008 financial crisis, see below.

Financial crises can bring wide ranging and unforeseen consequences beyond the stock market, and have a real impact on the economy, consumer confidence, and businesses.

During a financial sell-off market participants can become irrational and are driven to sell investments not based on fundamentals but are driven by fear, or a mania*! The additional selling pressure causes more selling, and the markets can quickly crash and wipe out the value of stocks (the opposite is true during a bull market when participants are driven by greed). The impacts of a financial crisis/crash are often long-term, with unintended consequences, global impacts, and can lead to a prolonged economic contraction (also see, 1929). Some important questions for consideration, will the stock market always be volatile, and crash? Is the stock market safe for investors? What will be the cause of the next sell-off? What can be learned from historical crises?

2008 Financial Crisis

Bad subprime mortgage loans and complex financial products contributed to the 2008 financial crisis. During August 2007, the $2 trillion subprime market collapsed, and Bear Stearns was the first big bank to fail during the crisis.[xvii]

Footnote:

*Financial crises/crashes are often associated with a mania or a panic by market investors.

On 25 September 2008 Lehman Brothers collapsed, it was a turning point in the crisis because of the complex financial products it traded like Credit Default Swaps CDS, and CDO Collateral Debt Obligations. The banking crisis that had started in the United States was suddenly a global financial crisis at this point.

In Europe banks also failed. In Iceland suffered a major setback when the nations banks collapsed due to the crisis, and required nationalisation (brought by the government). Northern Rock a United Kingdom bank had a bank run, and was also nationalised.

During the European banking crisis, that resulted in bank bailouts using public funds. For example: on January 15, 2009 Ireland nationalised Anglo Irish Bank, and on October 13, the British government bailed out Royal Bank of Scotland, Lloyds, and HBOS, according to *Credit Suisse (2015)*.

Footnote:

Credit Suisse, 2015, "Infographic, 2008-2014: Key Developments Post-Financial Crisis", via www.credit-suisse. com

The introduction of the Troubled Asset Relief Program or TARP, by the government was used to buy toxic debt. The $700 billion program passed in the House on October 3 2008. Quantitative easing was used to purchase US Treasuries. Questions of Moral Hazard were raised by market commentators with the use of bailouts for risky lending by banks.

The use of money printing and bank bailouts during the 2008 crisis, supported the recovery of stability to the markets, albeit driven by stimulus.

1929 Crash

Called "The Great Crash". The stock market had rallied for 9 years, before the NYSE started to fall in September and early October 1929. On Black Tuesday, October 29 1929, stock prices collapsed completely and 16,410,030 shares were traded on the New York Stock Exchange in a single day, and investors lost billions.[xviii]Following The Great Crash, came The Great Depression a period of low economic growth and high unemployment that lasted 10 years, unemployment reached a peak rate of 24.9% in 1933.[xix]

Further Crashes

Other recent significant financial market crashes include: the *Flash Crash* 2010, *Dot-Com Crash* 1999-2000, the 1997-98 *Asian Financial Crisis*, and the *Savings and Loan Crisis* 1986-1995.

For more reading on the subject of financial crises, and Wall Street history consider the following titles:

- *Wall Street: a history, Charles R. Geisst.*
- *The great crash, 1929, John Kenneth Galbraith.*

This chapter reviews important historical financial crises/sell-offs/panics, & crashes. Additional analysis of the 2008 financial crisis has been highlighted, and is important for evaluation the 2020 sell-off. Early market crises discussed included the Tulip crash, and the 1929 Great Crash.

8: 2022: A NASDAQ CORRECTION

Financial markets update, February 2022! The reversal in fortunes from the 2020 crash were short lived however as the markets started to decline again in 2022, and inflation rose impacting the U.S. economy. The Nasdaq Index recorded a market correction after falling from November 19 high to January 19, by -10.7% in 2022[xx]. In early 2022, the financial markets had started to fall again.

Author's note:

Some important developments have followed on from the 2020 financial markets crash, including the cryptocurrency crash in 2022, and the banking crisis of 2023. These are briefly mentioned as excerpts from my new book, *The Bank Sell-Off*, (see Appendix, v).

THANKS FOR READING *THE SELL-OFF ON WALL STREET*, BY B T

DON'T FORGET TO WRITE A REVIEW ON AMAZON!

More Books

***The Bank Sell-Off* by B T**

Read about the 2023 banking crisis. Inside readers will find out why four large U.S. banks failed. Plus, read about the 2022 cryptocurrency crash, and the demise of Credit Suisse bank.

APPENDIX

i) Use of Circuit Breaker

The Circuit Breaker were used to freeze stock markets in the United States on four occasions during March 2020, they are used following a more than -7% fall. Level 1, circuit meant that stock trading was halted for 15 minutes, to provide a pause in the trading. The circuit breakers were put in place by the Securities and Exchange Commission.

Dates circuit breaker used:

- Level 1, 03.09.2020
- Level 1, 03.12.2020
- Level 1, 03.16.2020
- Level 1, 03.18.2020

The effectiveness of the use of circuit breakers on the stock market was likely to have limited the drop on particular days they were used, but the degree of how useful such tools are for stopping an extended crash remain uncertain.

ii) **DJIA Percentage Change During Volatile Trading Feb-March 2020:**

- 03/12/2020, closing 21,200.62, percentage change -9.99%
- 03/13/2020, closing 23,185.62, percentage change +9.36%
- 03/16/2020, closing 20,188.52, percentage change -12.93%
- 03/24/2020, closing 20,704.91, percentage change +11.37%
  (Source: *S&P Dow Jones Indices*)

iii) Investments and Assets Performance in 2020

Gold has been used as a store of wealth for more than 5,000 years. Gold reached a 7 year high of $1,621.60 per ounce on February 20th, 2020.

Despite it's safe haven appeal, during March it sold off as investors sold gold too, the reason was possibly to raise cash for margin calls. Gold had similarly sold off in early 2008, before recovering. By 15 May 2020, Gold closed at $1,742 per ounce, reconfirming its safe haven status during a downturn. Gold traditionally holds its value or is likely to rise during a downturn, like a recession and offers investors a safe haven.

Bonds and treasuries came under selling pressure, see chart below S&P 500 Bond Index. The impact of the sell-off was widespread. The low yield of treasuries, a change in risk and inflation expectations, and the drop in short-term interest rates made these investments unattractive for the time. US Treasuries bonds are safe investments. The unfortunate news for investors is that they yield very little, if inflation increases then they will likely fall in value in real terms. Treasury yield curve in the United States as of May 2020, 10 year is 0.65%. The risks and benefits of Safe Haven investments during a financial crash were evidenced by these results in early 2020.

Volatility during trading was very high in February and March 2020, and this is shown by the VIX chart (see, Chart #2). The volatility in trading during Feb-March 2020 is highlighted below showing some of the most volatile trading days, with wild moves both up and down on the Dow Jones Industrial Average (DJIA). Bets on volatility (VIX Index) linked futures products during a market crash like 2020 delivered large returns for investors, as they spiked higher or lower as volatility increased, like the (TVIX) product.

iv) Questions & Answers for Students

Questions:

1. When did the financial markets crash in 2020?

2. What industries were least impacted by the financial crash?

3. How was the economy likely impacted by the 2020 financial crash?

4. What were some of the expected outcomes from stimulus spending?

5. What was the primary cause of the 2008 financial crisis?

6. Which Index on the U.S. stock market was the quickest to recover, and why?

7. How many times were Circuit Breakers used in March 2020, and why were they used?

8. Provide an example of a carry trade?

9. What are three safe-have investments?

10. What is a Bear market?

Answers:

1. February-March 2020

2. Biotechnology and the Information Technology industries

3. The economic growth was forecasted to decline and enter a recession in the United States

4. Inflation and a recovery for the financial markets

5. Housing debt defaults and complex financial products which spread the risk between financial institutions, and banks.

6. Nasdaq Index was the quickest to make a recovery, mostly due to technology stocks rising in value

7. At least 4 times in march 2020 in an attempt to slow the decline on financial markets and restore confidence

8. An example of the carry trade is to borrow in the Japanese Yen, with a low interest rate, and then to invest in the higher yielding U.S. treasuries to make a gain from the difference in interest rates

9. Gold, treasury bills, corporate bonds

10. A period of declining markets

v) **Excerpts from my new book, *The Bank Sell-Off* by B T:**

Cryptocurrency crash, 2022:

"In 2022 the cryptocurrency market crashed, and the failure of the UST & Luna tokens wiped out $40 billion in value within a short period but some estimates say $50-$60 billion according to the *Financial Times*, and it became known as the Terra Luna Crash, and the event lead to more cryptocurrency bankruptcies."

Banking crisis, 2023:

"During 2023 the banks in the United States and globally entered a sell-off. A number of medium and large banks failed or were taken over in the U.S. including First Republic Bank, Signature Bank, & Silicon Valley Bank. Credit Suisse, a 167-year-old Switzerland bank also collapsed, and entered a historic merger with its rival, UBS Group."

Credit Suisse failure, 2023:

"On Sunday March 19, 2023, it was announced that UBS Group, had agreed to a $3 billion Swiss francs ($3.25 billion) deal to buy Credit Suisse, with the Swiss National Bank offering to loan 100 billion Swiss francs ($108 billion), with the combined institution having $5 trillion in assets, based on reports by, *UBS*. A guarantee from the government also assumed up to $9 billion Swiss francs, it was done to "reduce any risks for UBS," according to a government announcement at the time. The combination of the two banks, was one of the largest deals in the global financial system in years. The tie-up was rushed through by regulators over the weekend to prevent a wider banking crisis, the tie-up with UBS Group gave the merged bank combined assets worth double as much as Switzerland's economy (GDP)."

EXHIBIT 1

The chart below shows the S&P 500 at an all time high 19 February 2020, then a dropping with a -12% correction by 27th February, the fastest crash -10% on record.

S&P 500 2020

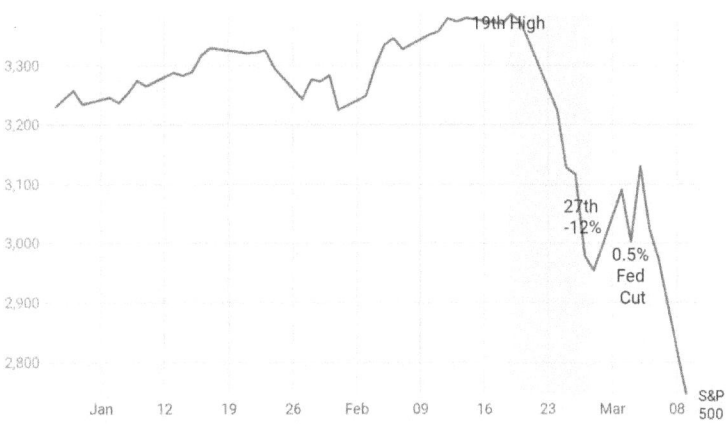

Chart: Author • Source: S&P Dow Jones Indices LLC. • Created with Datawrapper

EXHIBIT 2

The chart below shows the S&P 500 VIX Short term, it rose as the volatility in the markets rose fast.

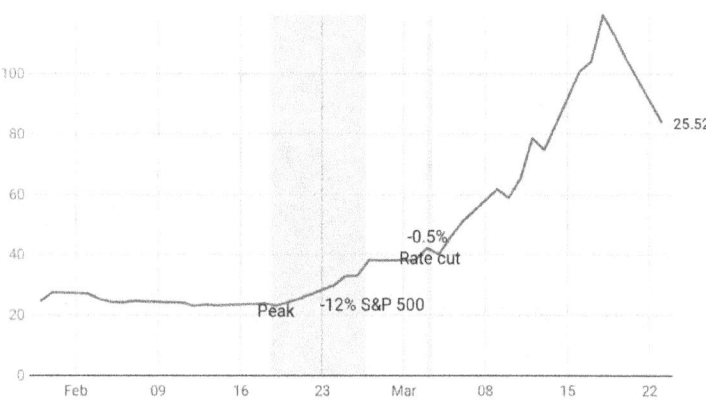

S&P 500 VIX Short-Term

Index MCAP
Chart: Author • Source: S&P Dow Jones Indices LLC • Created with Datawrapper

EXHIBIT 3

The chart below shows the DJIA as it entered a -20% bear market on March 11, 2020. Circuit breakers were used four times.

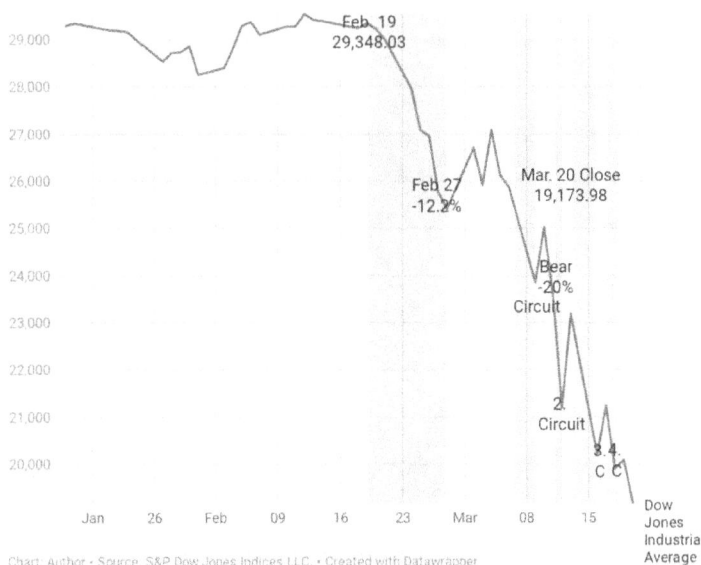

EXHIBIT 4

The chart below shows the S&P500 on a downward spiral, reaching a low on March 23, 2020 at 2,237 points. Federal Reserve rate cut -0.5%, WHO declaration, Fed funding announcement March 11. See Circuit breakers 1-4. National Emergency (NE).

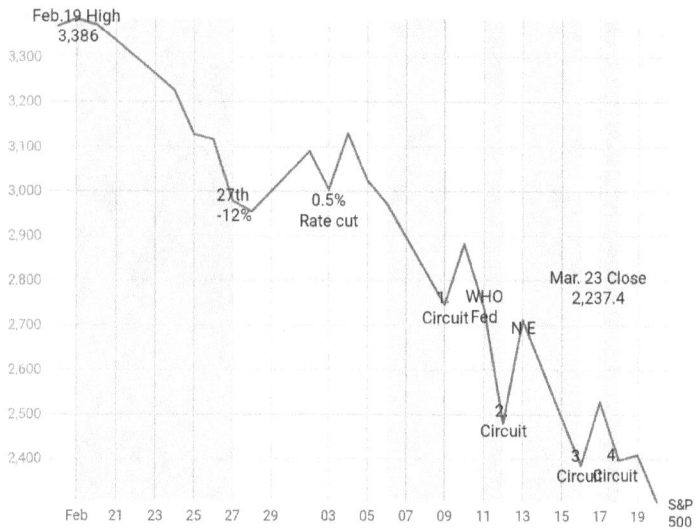

EXHIBIT 5

The chart below shows the S&P 500 Bond Index, bonds went up initially in February, but joined the sell-off in the March crash.

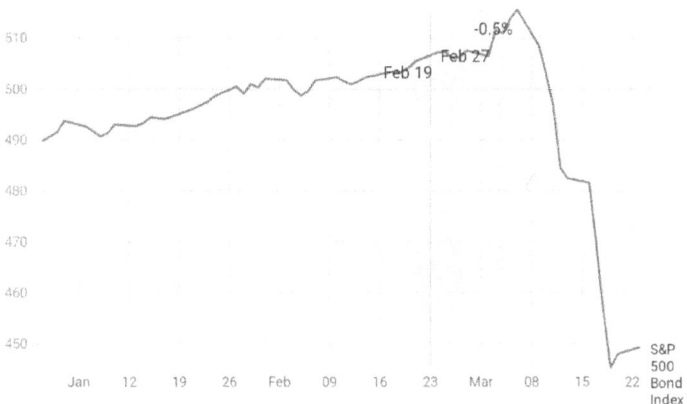

EXHIBIT 6

The chart above shows the S&P 500 rebounding in 2020.

S&P 500, 2020

Rebound from 23 March bottom.

S&P500: SPX

EXHIBIT 7

The chart above shows the DJIA rebounds from market lows.

EXHIBIT 8

Year to Date (YTD) for the S&P 500, 2020. Rebounds from lows.

S&P 500, 2020

YTD S&P 500.

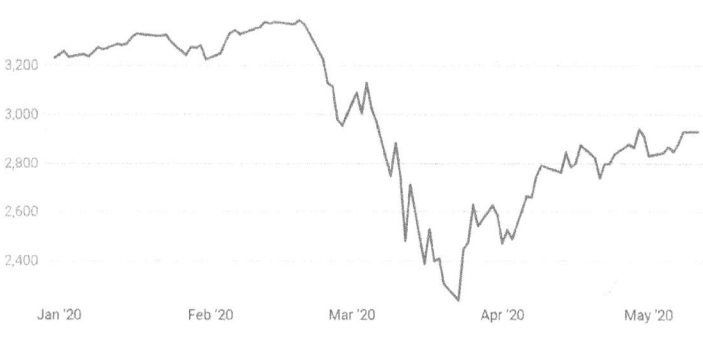

S&P500: SPX

Photo 1.
A facemask sold in Australia in 2020. Personal Protective Equipment (PPE) was in high demand and short supply. *Credit: Author.*

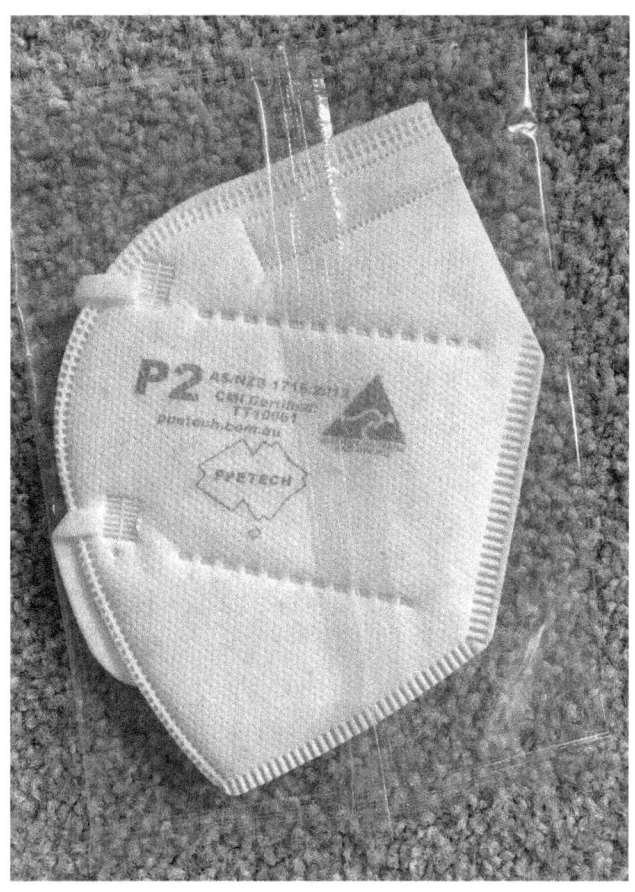

2. Credit Suisse stock price as seen in a trading app before the merger announcement with UBS, taken on Friday 17th March, 2023. Note: Market Cap is $7.92 billion. *Credit: Author.*

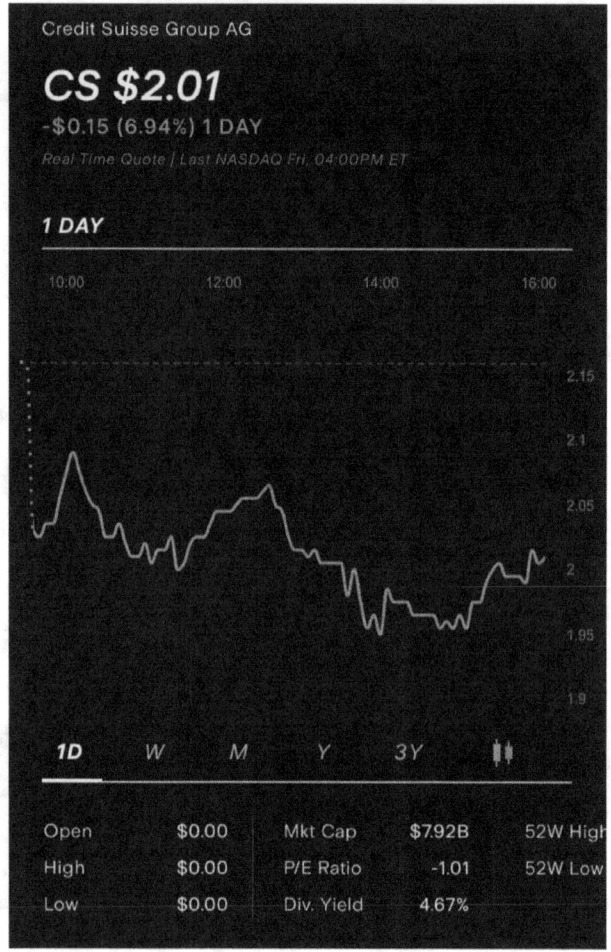

3. Credit Suisse 49 shares worth $98.49 USD, as seen in a trading app taken on Friday 17th March, 2023. Following the merger news over the weekend, on Monday the shares traded for below $1.

Credit: Author.

4. A Credit Suisse branch in gloomy weather, owned by UBS captured on November 30, 2023, Geneva, Switzerland. *Credit: BT*

5. A UBS branch. The merger with Credit Suisse in 2023 was one of the largest bank mergers. Photographed 17th, November 2023, Geneva. *Credit: Author.*

6. A UBS branch with sculpture. Photographed on 17th, November 2023, Geneva. *Credit: Author.*

#THE END#

ABOUT THE AUTHOR

The author has a commerce degree with a major in economics, and has worked in a number of different industries including event management, hospitality, and television.

BIBLIOGRAPHY

---

[i] Federal Reserve www.federalreserve.gov

[ii] Jeff Cox, "Here is everything the Fed has done to save the economy", CNBC, APR 13 2020

[iii] Erica Werner, "House democrats pass $3 trillion Coronavirus relief bill despite Trump's veto threat", The Washington Post, May 16, 2020

[iv] Interview, "Negative interest rates is not something we are considering" May 13, 2020. CNBC.

[v] see i

[vi] Matt Egan, "The US is becoming the king of debt. It's a neccesary risk", CNN Business, May 6, 2020

[vii] Jared Dillian, "Money is losing Its meaning", Bloomberg, April 15, 2020.

[viii] Ycharts, https://ycharts.com/indicators/us_m2_money_stock

[ix] Holtfrerich, Carl-Ludwig: The German inflation, 1914-1923

[x] Goldman Sachs, www.goldmansachs.com

[xi] Bureau Labour Statisticshttps://www.bls.gov/news.release/empsit.nr0.htm

[xii] Apple, www.apple.com

[xiii] "J.C. Penney Files for Bankruptcy", Yahoo Finance.

https://finance.yahoo.com/news/j-c-penney-files-bankruptcy-223255810.html

[xiv] Berkshire Hathaway
https://www.berkshirehathaway.com/reports.html

[xv] Diamond Princess https://en.wikipedia.org/wiki/COVID-19_pandemic_on_Diamond_Princess

[xvi] Phillip Inman, "Jolt to eurozone as German court warns against central bank stimulus", The Guardian May 5, 2020

https://www.theguardian.com/business/2020/may/05/jolt-to-eurozone-as-german-court-warns-against-central-bank-stimulus

[xvii] Sorkin Ross, Andrew, Too Big to Fail, Viking Penguin, 2009.

[xviii] History www.history.com

[xix] See xii

[xx] Reuters, "Wall Street sell-off deepens, Nasdaq confirms correction" https://www.reuters.com/business/futures-gain-unitedhealth-bofa-rise-results-2022-01-19/

www.ingramcontent.com/pod-product-compliance
Lightning Source LLC
Chambersburg PA
CBHW030048230526
45471CB00003B/999